D1799422

ISBN: 9781314567694

Published by:
HardPress Publishing
8345 NW 66TH ST #2561
MIAMI FL 33166-2626

Email: info@hardpress.net
Web: http://www.hardpress.net

he Wars of Cyru

1594

)ate of the first known edition, ... 1594

(B.M. C. 34, b. 15.)

Reproduced in Facsimile, 1911

The Tudor Facsimile Texts

[Vol. 133]

Under the Supervision and Editorship of

JOHN S. FARMER

The Wars of Cyrus

1594

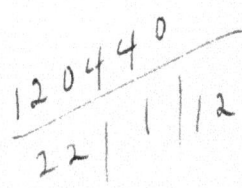

Issued for Subscribers by the Editor of

THE TUDOR FACSIMILE TEXTS

MCMXI

PR
2411
W2
1594a

The Wars of Cyrus.

1594.

The original of this facsimile is in deplorable condition (the photographer said it was, in common parlance, "a beast"), and is, with the next one to be issued, viz.: "The Wit of a Woman," one of the worst examples of early printing, both as regards the mechanical execution and the paper employed. The latter is thin, "cockled," and altogether inferior, whilst the condition of the copy may be gleaned at a glance from the title page, with its clever Museum bindery mendings. Indeed, so difficult and risky has been the process of reproduction, that in this case, as well as in that of "Wit of a Woman," the average has been two plates for each page; hence the fractional extra cost of this volume over and above the average 4½d. to 5d. per page usual in this series. I hope subscribers will forgive this little digression in a professedly purely bibliographical introduction.

In spite of these drawbacks the reproduction in facsimile is "distinctly good."

With "Wit of a Woman," ready December 30th, 1911, subscribers will receive a bound copy of the new Hand-book to the series without extra charge.

JOHN S. FARMER.

THE WARRES OF CYrus King of Persia, against Antiochus King of Assyria, with the Tragicall ende of Panthæa.

Played by the children of her Maiesties Chappell.

LONDON

Printed by E. A. for William Blackwal, and are to be sold at his shop ouer against Guild-hall gate. 1594.

The warres of Cyrus king of Persia against Antiochus king of Assiria.

Enter Cyrus, Histaspes, Chrysandus,
with other.

Cyrus.

YE Persians, Medians, and Hircanians,
Truslie assistans, assisters in this happie war,
Ye see the banded power of Asia,   (fields
Whose uumber ouerspread the Assirian
And in their passage dranke maine riu e s
By fauour of the gods, and our deuoire,   (dne
Are ouerthrowne and scattred through the plaines,
Like Autumne leaues before a Northren winde.
Cresus is foild, and fled to Lydia,
The Arabian prince is whelmde amidst the sands,
And last, the old Assyrian king is slaine.
Now triumph in the fortune of your hands,
Whose fame hath directed these affaires.
  Chris. O Cyrus when I saw the Lydian king,
Cresus that dastard and reproch of Asia,
Shining in armour forgde of Indian gold,
Braue mounted on a prauncer of Epetus.
So shamefully to forsake the field and flie,
I enuied that so cowardly a king,
Should vse so good an armour and a horse.
  Cyr. Chrisandas like to *Cresus* be our foes,

A   Glorious

Glorious in shew, but cowardly in minde.

Chris. Cyrus those armes which dastard Cresus were,
And horse of pride and courage past compare,
What heart so base that would deine to fight,
Might I but liue to backe so braue a steed.

Cyr. Cresus is gone, and gone with him his steed,
This with of yours Chrisantas is in vaine,
But of two hundred horses of mine owne,
Of gallant rase and courage singular,
Take you the choise and furniture withall,
The bridles bit of massie siluer wrought,
The bosses golde, the reynes of Persian silke,
The saddles all embrodered purple worke,
Armde through with plates, with fine ingrauen golde,
And golden trappers dangling to the ground.

Chris. So liue my Lord and flourish still,
As I regard this honourable gift.

Cyr. Now Lords we haue gotten the honor of the day,
And with our feet trod downe the Thrasian pride,
While I doe sacrifie for victorie,
and chose the holy aultars of the gods,
Doe you betwixt the armies part the spoiles,
and glad our men with fruits of our conquest.

Ara. What portion of the golde shall we reserue
To be employed in your highnesse vse?

Cyr. Araspas none for me, diuide it all,
It pleaseth me to see my souldiers rich. *Exit Cyrus.*

Chris. The Persian horse-men that did giue the charge
Shall haue fiue hundred talents for their share.

Hist. The Medians that did enforce the fight,
and seconded the Persian men at armes,
Allot to them six hundred arming coates.

Ara. The archers of Hercania serued so well,
as not to giue them paiment with the rest,
Were open wrong to their approude deserts.

You

Chr. You know that in the ſacking of Aſſyrians tents
we found three thouſand Scithians bowes in ſtore,
finiſht with quiuers readie to the field,
Let them be lotted to the Hercanians part.

Hiſt. And truth *Chriſantas* you know well,
That bowes and quiuers gree with archers beſt,
Cyrus himſelfe you ſee refuſeth golde,
And onely ſeekes to make his fellowes rich,
what reſtes amidſt the conquered ſpoiles,
wherein his highneſſe may be gratified?

Ara. *Hiſtaſpis* there is a proud Aſſyrian tent,
Wherein the king was wont to ſleepe and banket in,
I thinke if that were offered to his hands,
Cyrus would take it in moſt gracious part.

Chr. But is the pride and brauerie thereof,
worthie to be preſented to our Lord?

Araſ. Aſia hath not ſeene a richer priſe,
The couering is of blew Sydonian ſilke,
Imbrodered all with pearle and precious ſtones,
They glimmer brighter than the Sunne it ſelfe,
On euerie point of the pauilion,
There ſtandes a princely top of Phenix plumes,
which trickt with ſpangles and with ſiluer belles,
And euerie gentle murmur of the winde,
delights the day with euerie harmonie.
The ſtakes where with it is faſtened to the ground,
are maſſie ſiluer of the pureſt proofe,
The ropes are all of chrimſon ſilke and golde,
Hung from the top with wreſts of iuorie,
Vnder a Vine where Bacchus brniſeth grapes,
and twentie cubits houer in the leaues,
Beleeue me Lords, when I beheld the thing,
The worke appeardeſo glorious to the eie.

Chr. *Araſp* as you deſcribe a princely thing,
Worthie to be preſented to a king.

A   **And**

Hist. And here is a tent, though far from such a tent,
This shall be mine, the owner's fled or slaine,

Cri. O beautie rare, and more than mortall shape,
What goddesse oweth this earthly tabernacle.

Pan. *Nicasia* sings while *Panthea* sits and sighes.
But singing sings of *Pantheas* wretchednes.

Chris. What are ye Ladie?

Pan. What I would not be.

Chris. Faire you are, what would ye more?

Pan. I would be free.
Ye Persian Lords I am a wofull dame,
Exposed to wretchednesse and fortunes wrath,
And thus I haue resolude you what I am.

Ara. Ladie, the graces that adorne your presence,
Deserues a fortune milde as is your face.
But howsoeuer Fortune enuies you,
Yet we will vse you honourable still.

Pan. You vse me then but as you ought to doe.

Chris. Nay Ladie we may vse you otherwise,
For voluntarie fauours be no debt.

Pan. But Lords what ere you ought is debt,
you ought to vse me well, and therefore debt.

Ara. Madam, you are a captiue in our hands,
And captiues are not to command the conquerours.

Pan. No Lords, if captiues might command the con-
I would command you to release me hence. (querors,
But captiue as I am, honour commands,
That you intreate and vse me honourably.

Chris. Such honour as to captiues doth belong,
Such honour Ladie we intend to you.

Pan. My sex requireth more then common grace.

Ara. And eke so doth it that liuely face.

Pan. Let be my vsage as shall please my conquerou,
And now Ile learne to craue with seruile tearmes,
My lords, though captiue, yet I am a Queene,

And

And wife vnto the absent Susan king.
My lord and heare Assyrian Abradate,
And noble prince and mightie man at armes.
Vpon ambassage of the king of Batria.

Chr. But madam what persuasion moou'd your
To thrust your self vnto the Assyrian campe.   (mind,

Pan. Weying the double fortune of the warres,
And in my thoughts foredreading these mishaps,
What likelier rescue to preuent my harmes,
Then to be garded with a mightie campe,
Since that an armie of vnited hearts,
Is stronger then a fort af brazen walles.

Ara. Madam, your fall is great and lamentable,
Thus of a Queene a captiue to become,
This rests to shew your princely fortitude,
In bearing these mishaps with patient minde.

Pan. Philosophy hath taught me to embrace,
A meane and moderation in mishaps,
Long since I learnde to master all affects.
And perturbations that assaile the minde,
Onely I haue not learnde to master chaunce,
yet haue I learnde to scorne the vtmost spight,
Onely the pangue that most torments my thought,
Is absence of my best beloued lord.

Chris. Learne henceforth to forget your lord,
There liues an other lord to enioy your loue,
Victorious *Cyrus* he shall be your lord.

Pan. Victorious *Cyrus* though I be his thrall,
Shall know my honour is inuincible.

Ara. But they that once in state of bondage bee,
Must yeeld to hest of others that be free.

Pan. Lords deeame of me or *Cyrus* as you please,
Onely this outward person is his thrall,
My minde and honour free and euer shall.

Chris. For that agree with *Cyrus* as you may,

LnA   Till

Till then *Gaspas* take her to your tent.

Aras. Come Ladie, you must walke apart with me,

Pan. So fortune and my destinies agree.

Enter Gobrias and his page.

Go. Persians conduct me to your generall.

Chr. What art thou that thus armde with sword and

Dares craue accesse vnto our generall? (speare.

Go. I come to yeeld, bring me to *Cyrus* tent.

Hist. Thy habit showes thou art an enemie,

And we may suspect thou meanest but ill.

Therefore if thou wilt yeeld vnarme thy selfe,

And we will bring thee vnto *Cyrus* tent.

Go. The Assyrian king whom ye haue put to death,

Making me leader of a thousand horse,

Buckled the armour with his gracious hands,

Nor shall it be vnloosed but by a king.

Hist. How hautie minded is this conquered man,

Cyrus shall know vpon what tearmes he standes,

Assyrian captaine as thou louest thy life,

Stand not vpon thy guard, but yeeld to vs.

Go. Smal guard haue I to shield me from your swords,

Most of my region is slaine in fight,

And of a thousand onely these are left,

Whose wounds yet bleeding proues the faint & weak,

Yet rather will we runne vpon your speares,

Then with dishonour yeeld our weapons,

These if ye iniure vs must be our friends,

And either make vs liue or die with them.

Ile yeeld to kill

Enter Cyrus.

Cyr. Of whence art thou that craues addresse to vs?

Go. By birth great *Cyrus* an Assyrian,

And

And of the noble stoure in Babylon
Sometime commander of a thousand horse.
But those thy men thou hast slaughtered and despised,
And therefore I haue lost the ample field,
yet I am mightie Gobrias, rich in reuenues, strong in for-
That can command a campe of fighting men, (tresses
As resolute (be it said without offence)
As those that haue the vse of their vpon mine oath.
All which with me the gouernor of all,
I yeeld vnto your mightie patronage.

Cyr. This stout Assyrian hath a liberall looke,
And of my soule is faire free from basenesse,
Albeit Gobrias I mistrust thee not,
yet tell me being so valiant and so strong,
Why rather yeeld'st thou to thy enimie,
Then liue with freedome in Assyria.

Gob. O know my lord, whilest the Assyrian king,
Which in this warre was slaine, enioyed the crowne,
Being highly fauoured of his maiestie,
He sent vnto me for mine onely sonne,
Meaning to grace me with the nuptiall
Of his faire daughter louely Cumila,
I glad to haue alyance with the king,
Sent him my sonne. Who comming to the court,
Was faire entreated, gently entertained,
And well was he that might be his copers,
For faire he was and full of sweete demeanour.
Pleasant, sharpe, wise and liberall,
And were he not my sonne, I would say more,
Though his remembrance makes me weepe outright.

Cyr. Noble Assyrian either leaue to weepe,
Or speake no more, Cyrus is full of ruth,
And when a man of thy estate laments,
He cannot chuse but weepe for companie,
Drie vp these teares and tell the rest,

B   Began

Gob. ...gan to grow familiar with my countrey,
And with him rode a hunting in the woods,
where first the hounds put vp a russet beare,
At which the king floong soone his hunting dart,
And missed. But mine threw and pearced his heart.
Then sodainly a Lion did arise,
At whom likewise he let his Iauelin flie,
And hit him not, which when my sonne perceyude,
He ouerthrew the Lion as the beare,
which done, said he, twice haue I throwne and sped,
whereat the prince snatcht from his page a speare,
And in a rage murdered my guiltlesse sonne,
And that (which greeueme more) when he was dead,
Albeit the old king wept most bitterly,
He neither did repent nor sheda teare,
Nor would consent to giue him buriall,
but left him in the field votill I came,
And tooke his bodie in these aged armes,
which eke for griefe made me to let him fall,
And then a fresh made him to bleed againe,
And me to weepe vpon his naked breast.
Oh iudge my lord, if you haue had a sonne,
How heauily I brooke his timelesse death.
Oh iudge my lord, whether that I haue cause
To offer seruice to that murtherer,
On whom I cannot looke, but in his face,
as in a glasse I see my slaughtered sonne.

Cyr. Gobrius thou hast iust cause to reuolt,
And we to trust thy welcome vnto vs,
And for the thousand horse which thou hast lost,
we will require them with a greater gift,
Be thou lieutenant of the Arthanians.

Gob. I humblie thanke your royall maiestie,
And here in presence of the Persian lords,
adopt you heire of all my prouinces.

B   My

My holdes and caſtels, villagis and townes,
Conditionally that I may be reuenged,
On this archtyrant murderer of my ſonne,
Sauing one daughter I haue neuer a child,
And ſhe endued with iewels plate and golde,
Shall be beſtowed as you my lord think beſt.

Cyr. Aſſirian I haue captaines worthie here,
She ſhall be matched as beſeemeth a princes borne,
And for reuenge vpon the Aſſirian king,
We will girt in Babylon with our high hoſt,
Or either ſtarue them with a lingring ſiege,
Or rip his bowels with our Perſian ſwords,
But in the meane time ſtalike in our tent,
His ſafetie lead the Aſſyrian to our campe,
And entertaine him as beſeemeth a prince,
Arcybas and Chriſantus follow him,
Wherefore my lord giue it in charge,
And will you, preſently,
Is all the ſpoile diuided equally,

Ann. It is my Lord, and euerie ſouldier pleaſed,
Where is enclaſed a iewell of ſuch worth,
As Aſia hardly can afoord the like,
The Sofian king ſhot, Abradaſts Queene,
A woman ſo richly imbelliſhed,
with beautie and perfection of the minde,
As neuer any mortall creature did,
Her haire as radient as is Tagis ſand,
And ſofter than the ſtreame on which it runned,
Her lillie cheekes all died with ruddie bluſh,
Caſtes ſuch reflection to the ſtanders by,
As doth the vnion of ten thouſand ſunnes,
Through her tranſparent necke the fire doth play,
And makes it fairer then a Chriſtall glaſſe,
And from her eye it ſeemes nature herſelfe,
Bids euerie ſtarre receiue his proper light,
For with her glorie ſhe caſtes ſuch a brightneſſe,

As makes the euening more cleere hied than the day,
And day more fayre ... ...
But when she walkes so pleasid in her voice,
As were she blacker when it keepit his night,
She would be faire to hat ... ...
Or wildest Satyr Man in you thight in the campe,
And when she lookes openi your were she dumbe
Her beautie were a feend of cleopatra ...
And had she neither louelinesse nor wit,
The harmonie that makes would rauish you,
She weepes complaine of h ld ... that ... the sing
And sighes ... that note,
Which Orpheus sung for ... ...
with wringed hands her euening in his keepe ...
Vpon their mournefull breast as were we then,
we could not chuse but melt to heare their songs,
wherefore my lord comfort ould your tale thing,
And with your presence ... ...
Cyr. ... ... hued my visit her
when by her ... only be comforted ...
Ara. Your Grace ... pleade of her, and yet not louse.
Cyr. Dost ... thinke that loue is violent?
Ara. Nay rather volume the say gratious lord,
you know that woman beauide ... ... fire,
And fire doth alwayes burne all thing alike,
Therefore if nature were of such great power,
Should euerie man by beautie be enflamed,
But beautifull things are euer in equall power,
For some loue this which other doe disdaine,
Either for feare or ... doe not thē enioy,
The sister ... ... now long ...
The daughter ... ... not defired,
And yet some loue haue any of them both,
Cyr. If loue be volume it as thou saist,
why ... loued lad defire he all they will.

H   The

Ara. They may...

Cyr. Haue you not seene others weepe and waile for
  death?
Emptie their purse of coine, their braine of wit,
Sending both gifts and letters to their loues?

Ara. They yeeld too much vnto affection,
T'is follie and not beautie makes them...

Cyr. Men are in folly when they are in loue,
Vrge me no more, I will not visite her,
For by the eie loue slips into the heart,
Making men idle, negligent...
Nothing can more dishonour warriours...
Then to be conquered within womans...
Araspas I resigne my part to thee,
Thou shalt be keeper of this Susan Queene,
Vse her as...
Excuse me for not...
Bid her be merrie...
And say that *Cyrus* will... *Exeunt.*

Enter Cres... and Nobles.

Nob. *Antiochus* king of Assyria,
So Lord of Euphrates and Babylon,
How long wilt thou lament thy fathers death,
Cast off those mourning weedes...

Another. How long will I lament my fathers death,
Vntill proud Persia... *Cyrus* death.

Cres. Oh...
So strong... were not Babylon,
Fortified with...
Garded with...
Sooner would...
Then you with open...

                                What

Ant. What is reuenge but open warres,
As were *Antiochus* a priuate man,
And one of you king of Affyria,
I would not faile to worke his ouerthrow,
But you that are not touch't with inward griefe,
will not in that attempt be refolute.

Cef. Vouchfafe O Lord to tell me what it is,
If I attempt it not then let me die.

Ant. Why this it is, feigne I haue iniurde thee,
And offer feruice to the Perfian king,
Then being receiued as late *Gobrias* was,
How eafie maift thou flea him and efcape,
For in the night he walkes about his campe,
Without a guard euen as a common man.

Cef. Yet he that killes him fure is to die.

Ant. I thought the feare of death would daunt him
A thoufand talents would I freely giue,
To him that vndertakes this enterprife.

Cef. My Lord I am refolude, giue me the gold,
And I will venture life in this exploit.

Ant. My treafurer at armes fhall giue it thee,
And *Ctififon* when I receiue his head,
Befide this fumme thou fhalt haue annuall pay,
As much as thy reuenues mount vnto,
And where thou art by calling but a knight,
Ile make thee Lord of many prouinces.

Cref. As for the gold keepe it till I returne,
and if I die deliuer it to my friend.

Ant. Well *Ctefiphon* manage this glorious act,
Let me embrace him ere I take my leaue.

Cref. Fare well my lord. Now you Affyrian gods,
To whom we facrifice our fo-mens blood,
Giue fauour to my lookes, faith to my fpeach,
That being gracious with the Perfian Lord,
By me Affyria may be free from bands,

And

And both the king and subiects death reuengde,

Nob. Fare well braue minded *Cresiphon.*

Ant. While this is doing we will march from hense,

Vnto the countrey where *Gobrias* dwelt,

He hath a cattell well replenished,

with vittailes, men and furniture,

And as our spies giues vs to vnderstand,

His onely daughter stayes within the hold,

Not knowing of her fathers late reuolt,

Therefore will we surprise her vnawares,

and thou shalt be lieutenant in his stead,

when we haue made his souldiers yeeld the fort.

Enter Araspas solus.

Ara. Must I confesse that loue is violent.

By doting on my captiue *Panthea,*

I will not loue. Ile bridle those affects,

I cannot be resisted, I must yeeld,

Oh what a tyrant is this cruel loue,

That drinkes my blood, and makes me pale and wan,

That sucks my spirits, and makes me weake and faint,

That teares my heart, and makes me almost dead,

That reuels in my braines and makes me mad,

I am a souldier, and will conquer loue,

Ile mount me straight, giue me a horsmans staffe,

Proud loue, sit fast, for now *Araspas* runnes,

Runne and scarcely stand: O *Panthea,*

Thou sets my idle fantasie thus a worke,

and makes me speake and thinke I know not what.

I would I might forget faire *Panthea,*

I cannot name her but I must say faire,

And that word faire makes me remember her,

Panthea is vglie, but ile ill fauoured foule,

And who is so beautifull as she,

Ant.

And I must weepe for this minister my...
Why should a weepe alleou: be red foorwhat...
I... abaide my dieu, we can not but die...
Die not but liue and enioy my loue...
What contrarietie consisteth in my wordes...
O reconcile them, louely *Panthea*...
Thy lookes hath made me harde like...
...his onely daughter slaine with...

Enter Panthea and Nicasia.

Therefore get we hence for...

Pan. I haue intelligence that our Lord dislickd, but
we come to comfort him as...

Aras. Oh welcome *Panthea*, shall I tell my griefe?
Pan. Sit still my Lord, &...
why change you colour thus, what troubles you?
Aras. Something stands by and whispers in my eare,
A kisse of *Panthea* will recouer me...
Pan. O leaue these idle wordes, they make you worse
Ara. Nay they recouer me, I am halfe well...
Pan. So say they that are going from the world.
Ara. *Panthea* sit downe, but sit so *Panthea*,
As I may view thy face, oh else I die...
Pan. *Nicasia* command the musicke play,
It may be musicke will allay the fit...
Ara. *Nicasia* cause the musicke ceasse, *Musick plaid.*
For it is harsh and mars the harmonie...
Come *Panthea* sit downe by me, and let vs talke.
Pan. Talke is... sleepe.
Aras. Oh looke...
Panthea haue naid thy Lord a souldier and loue-sicke
Aras. I cannot keepe it in, and burnd my heart...
For thee sweete *Panthea*...
Pan. For me, my Lord...
Aras. Fling not away celestiall *Panthea*,
Though I were halfe dead I should behold thee...

The

Pan. The aire will hurt thee, whither wilt thou go,

Ara. Where *Panthea* goes, oh frowne not my faire
loue.

Pan. Then loue me not, elfe I will more then frowne.

Ara. What will a captiue woman threat her loue.

Pan. Oh giue poore *Panthea* leaue to thret her felfe.
I meane my Tragedie fhall end the loue.

Ara. No louely Queene, Ile rather end my loue,
Then anger *Panthea*, much lefle let her die,
And yet God knowes my loue can neuer end,
Being infinite in meafure and in time.

Pan. What wordes bee thefe that cut my eares with
Oh *Abradates* little doft thou know, (griefe,
What miferie poore *Panthea* doth fuftaine,
wicked *Araspas* perifh in thy loue.   *Exit Panthea.*

Aras. Cannot I winne her, O vnhappie man?
Araspas thou wantft eloquence to wooe,
Againft chaftitie no eloquence preuailes,
It was becaufe I offered her no gift,
She is a Queene what gifts can compaffe her,
I fhould haue courted her with better words,
But here doth loue and threatning difagree,
Nothing but Magicke can obtaine her loue,
If Magicke will, then *Pamb* a fhall be mine.

Actus fecundus. Enter *Hiftaspis* and *Chrifantas.*

Hift. *Chrifantas*, when I looke into the life,
The maners, deeds, and qualities of minde,
The grauenefle, power, and imperiall parts,
wherewith yong *Cyrus* is fo full adornde,
My thoughts forefee that he is ordained of God,
To enlarge the limits of the Perfian raigne.

Chr. *Hiftaspis*, rare it is to fee thofe yeeres,
So furnifhed with fuch rare experience,
As is not common in the grayeft haires,
Befides his bodie hath of thefe rare gifts.

C   Vfed

Vſed to labour, hunger, thirſt and colde,
Giues true foretokens that the prince will proue,
A famous warriour and a conquerour.

Hiſt. And of the ſundry vertues that abounds
Dayly increaſing in her princely breaſt,
Religion to the gods exceedes them all.

Cbr. And reaſon good for of all humane workes,
The care of them ſhould chieflie be preferred.

Enter Cyrus

Cy. Is this Aſſyrian friend or foe to vs,
That dares approch ſo neare the Perſian campe.

Cre. In bending of my ſpeare to Babylon,
And breaking it againſt the Aſſyrian ground,
I came a friend, not foe to Cyrus campe.

Hiſt. What reaſon moues thee an Aſſyrian borne,
To beare ſuch rancour to thy countrey ſoyle.

Cre. That ſecret I reſerue for Cyrus eares,
Vnto whoſe ſecret fauour, I ſubmit
My perſon, honour, fortune, fame and life.

Hiſt. Informe the king certainly I will.
O Perſians truely fortunate are you,
Vnder ſubiection of ſo ſweete a prince,
That meaſures all the actions of his life,
By mercie, iuſtice, and reſpect of right.

Hiſt. It ſeemes th'Aſſyrian prince hath iniured this
with ſome notorious great indignitie. (man.

Cy. Man of Aſſyria, what wouldſt thou with me?

Cte. O gracious Lord great and inuincible,
Receiue into protection of your grace,
A wretched man vndone by tyrannie,
And lawleſſe rigour of a cruell prince.

Cy. What prince is he that thou accuſeſt thus?

Cte. The new Aſſyrian king, a man diſtainde

With

With endlesse markes of villanie and blood.

Cy. Discend vnto the purpose of thy tale,
And make thy state and fortune plaine at once.

Cte. I am, (I am said I) I was a man,
Earst noble, now banisht reprobate,
Highlie in fauour with the Assyrian prince,
Till sensuall rage of his vnbrideled lust,
Did lay my state and honour in the dust,
And thus great Lord begun my Tragedie,
One onely virgin daughter had your thrall,
Of yeares inclining now to mariage state,
Her face and beautie (if I seeme not vaine)
were equall to the best Assyrian dames,
And she supposde the flower of Babylon.
The bruite of which her rare perfections ran,
Swifter than Fame through all th'Assyrian land,
And lastly rested in the princes eares,
Who wounded with report of beauties pride,
Vnable to restraine his moderne desire,
Attended by a band of armed men,
Inuades my castell when I was at rest,
And bare my daughter thence with violate hands,
Vnto his pallace where she doth remaine,
As concubine allotted to his bed,
Striuing her desperate honour to preserue,
I came in frantike sort to Babylon,
Exclaiming on this villainous despite,
Banding the prince with many a bitter view,
My iust complaint when once he vnderstood,
He sortes me out a damned bloudie crew,
Of ruffians, slaughterers, murderers, and theeues,
Professed men for gaine and lucre sake,
To make no conscience whom they slay and kill,
Those men by solemne othe had vowed my life,
A sacrifice vnto their cursed so order,

C 2   And

And houre by houre they fought to reaue my soule,
Liuing in hazard of continuall death,
I knew no hope for me at Babylon,
Other then my graue and dumlesse sepulchre,
And so for refuge to my wretched life,
I haue abandoned countrey, friends and all,
And prostrate my estate at _Cyrus_ feete,
O puissant Lord whose great and conquering sworde,
was forgde by _Mars_, and made for victorie,
Protect the life of thy vnhappie thrall,
And make him follower of the Persian armes,
That in the fortune of thy mightie hand,
The fall of _Cresiphon_ may be reuengde.

  Gob. O _Cresiphon_, this tale of thine reuiues
The wofull memorie of my dearest sonne,
Slaughtered by that most barbarous tyrant hand.

  Cyr. _Gobrias_ ye haue heard the Assyrian tale,
What great complaints he makes against the prince,
And those not causelesse if his wordes be true,
Now _Cyrus_ is not rashly credulous,
Nor bindes his faith on euerie strangers vowes,
Tell me _Gobrias_, dost thou simplie thinke,
That this discourse is naught but naked truth,
Or else some forged or dissembled glose,
To sound our secrets, and bewray your drifts.

  _Go._ _Cyrus_ the disposition of this prince,
Solde vp and sworne to endlesse villanies,
May proue the griefes of _Cresiphon_ vnfained,
Vpon my conscience _Cyrus_ trust the man,
No doubt his sorrow and complaints are true.

  Cre. O _Cyrus_ so it pleasde the immortall Gods,
How happie were thy seruant, if his words
proceeded from a vaine dissembling tongue,
So were my daughters honor vndefiled,
And _Cresiphon_ her father not exiled.

                                    Be

Cyr. Be valiant *Ctefiphon* and follow me,
Follow the fortune of a haphie campe,
Not doubt thou, but thou shalt fee the ende,
Shall rue the iniuries of his barbarous life,
Among the damned foules in darkeft hell.

   Cre. Then fhould my ghoft with feafeleffe wordes
     oppreft.
Paffe and difcend into the graue in reft.

                        Exeunt omnes.

             To the audience.
  We gentle gentlemen deuife of late,
To fhunne the vulgar and the vertuous,
Prefent to you worthie to iudge of vs,
Our workes of woorth and valiantnes at once.
What wants in vs imagin in the workes,
What in the workes condemne the writer of,
But if the worke and writing pleafe you both,
That Zenophon from whence we borrow write,
Being both a fouldier and philofopher,
Warrants what we record of *Panthea*,
It is writ in fad and tragicke tearmes,
May moue your teares then you content, our mufe
That feemes to trouble you againe with toies
Or needleffe antickes, imitations,
Or fhewes, or new deuifes fpring a late,
we haue exilde them from our Tragicke ftage,
As trafh of their tradition, that can bring
nor inftance, nor excufe. For what they do
In ftead of mournefull plaints our Chorus fings,
Although it be againft the vpftart guife,
Yet warranted by graue antiquitie,
we will reuiue the which hath long beene done.

                           Exit.

Enter Alexandra like a page, Libanio in Alexan-
dras apparell.

Lib. Madame you see your page doth vndertake,
A costly peece of seruice for your sake,
For well that seruice costly may be called,
The ende whereof of force must cost my life;
For when th'Assyrian king shall vnderstand
My forged habit, and dissembling sex,
And in these female weedes shall find *Libanio*,
And *Alexandra* freely scapt his handes,
What hope but certaine death remaines for me,
And that with torments rare and exquisite,
Yet madame for the reuerence to my Lord,
And dutie that doth bind me to your selfe,
I will be *Alexandra* for this once,
and die to saue your honour and your life.
Alex. O trustie seruant, seruant of such faith,
Worthie to attend the person of a god,
Rather then daughter of poore *Gobrias,*
This sacred seruice to a silie dame,
Shall be ingrauen in tables of my heart,
with letters and charecters so perfourmed,
That when this bodie is bestow'd in graue,
No time nor yet corruption shall deface,
The print thereof from *Alexandras* breast.
Lib. Thankes Ladie, And for your further meede,
Sufficeth me the honour of the deede,
Me thinkes I see the Assyrian tyrant at hand,
Now madame arme your couragious hart,
And trust your page for *Alexandras* part.
Alex. A Tragicall part, feare *Libanio*

Enter Antiochus, Seleucus, Critobulus with
others.

Bi3

Ant. Bird of a traitor I presumde at last,
Your lot would be to light into my handes,
Although of cankred heart you would not yeeld,
Vntill your castell shaked about your eares.

Lib. O soueraigne Lord stand gracious to this dame,
That neuer trespast in offence to you.

Ant. Thy fathers treason in reuolting backe,
From due alleageance to th'Assyrian crowne,
I will reuenge vpon his daughters life.

Lib. What honour in a sillie virgins death,
That nere had power or will to harme your grace.

Ant. Because the plants of such corrupted stocke,
will fructifie according to the roote,
And for *Gabrio* treason to his prince,
I will preuent like mischiefes in his case.

Lib. Admit *Gabrio* might be reclaimed,
And bring them to my Lord,
Would you reuiue then
And take him to your former grace againe.

Ant. So let the gods
Rewarding those
And firme his faith and loyaltie to me.

Lib. Then promise before you, wreake reuenge on me,
Grant passeport and safe conduite
See where he come and giue it him,
The desperate
When once my father
And that my life
I know that instant howre be will returne,
And yeeld himselfe
Suborne me

Ant. Scribe giue her
And boy when you arriue before *Gabrios*,
Tell if he returne I pardon him,
If otherwise, off goes his daughters head.

Alex. I will dread Lord: O madam grant she goth

The se

Thefe eyes once more may fee your libertie.

                           Exit Alexander.

Lib. As pleafeth their dieties *Libanio.*

Ant. *Dinon* take you this damfell to your charge,
And vfe her noblie though fhe be a thrall.

Dinon To vfe her worfe the honour were but fmall.

                           Exeunt omnes.

      Enter Ctefiphon.

  Cte. I murther *Cyrus*, farre be fuch a thought,
Much more the execution of the deed,
Like as the Sunne beames to the gazers eye,
So is his view to daunted *Ctefiphon*,
During the rancor of my wicked minde,
And melting all in thoughts of fweet remorfe,
How wife and gracious is this Perfian king,
Who by his wifdome winnes his followers hearts,
Letting them march in armour wrought with gold,
And he girt in a coate of complete fteele:
O *Cyrus* politique and liberall,
How honourable and magnanimious,
Rewarding vertue, and reuenging wrongs,
How full of temperance and fortitude,
Daring to menace Fortune with his fworde,
Yet mercifull in all his victories, *Enter Cyrus.*
See where he comes, Ile falle vpon the ground,
And afke for pardon at his highneffe feet.

  Cyr. Rife vp Affyrian, *Cyrus* is no God,

  Cte. O *Cyrus*, know my Lord,
My Lord, faid I, no I will renounce him quite,
Subornd me wretch with his perfuafious wordes,
To doe a deed of fuch impietie,
As I God know wes fuborne to thinke vpon,
It was thy death victorious *Cyrus*,
But mightie Lord your vertues conquered me,
And of an enemie falfe and trecherous,

                              Am

Am I become a vowed friend to *Cyrus* health,
And in that resolution prest to die.

Cyr. Liue long to waile for thy pretended ill,
As free from punishment as for reward,
The liues of kings are garded by the gods,
Nor are they in the hands of mortall men,
Assyrian, though thy sword were at my breast,
The gealous angell that attends on vs,
Would snatch it from thy hands, and fling it downe.
And therefore muse not at this accident.

Cte. Seeing knightly Cyrus is thus mercifull,
Vouchsafe this seruice at thy vassals hands,
Giue me but letters from your Maiestie,
To signifie how faine your would haue peace,
And draw your legions from Assyria,
And bearing them vnto *Antiochus*,
In the deliuerie I will murther him.
So highly do I honour Cyrus name,
So vildlie thinke on base *Antiochus*.

Enter Gobrias with Alexandra.

Cyr. Thou shalt haue letters to th'Assyrian king,
Free libertie to passe from this our campe,
And conduit monie from our Treasurie,
Attend our leysure, I will send thee straight.
What virgin is it that *Gobrias* leades?

Go. My daughter mightie Cyrus, and your child,
For I commit her to your patronage.

Cyr. Then princely virgin welcom to our campe.
But why sigh you, why hang you downe the head?
And in your pale lookes burie beauties pride,
T'is pitie these lookes should be stainde with teares.

Alex. Euen as a doue late rifeled by the Eagle,
Whose breast is tainted with his forked talents,
So stands poore *Alexandr* terrified.

An

And almost dead to think of her escape,
If thou be *Cyrus* of whom Asia rings,
Rescue, O rescue poore *Libanio*.

   Cyr. From whom faire madame should I rescue him.
   Alex. O from Antiochus that bloodie king.
Who when he heard my father serude your grace,
Besiegde his fortresse with his men at armes,
Where onely I and that *Libanio* staide,
By whom I liue; For when the hold was lost,
He being bondman and of a baser birth,
would needes constraine me to put on his weedes,
And he disguisde as I was woont to go,
would be *Gobrias* daughter in my stead;
And so was thought of king Antiochus,
and all the nobles of his warlike campe,
But I a bondman and at his request,
whose care was onely to preserue my life,
Sent hither as a messenger from him,
To will my father whom they thought my Lord,
To leaue your campe, and come to Babylon,
Or else *Libanio* his beloued childe
should die for his so traitorlike reuolt,
And die he must, least *Cyrus* giue him life.
   Cyr. The deed was full of honor and deceit,
If gold will pay his raunsome, he shall liue,
And therefore *Alexandra* be not sad,
   Gob. So shall *Gobrias* be at *Cyrus* becke,
And for his sake make lauish of his blood.
   Alex. And when they know how he deluded them,
I feare theyle rate his raunsome at his head.
   Cy. Then blood and death Bellonas waiting maid,
shall ghastly march in Babylons waste streetes,
And neuer was a bondmans death reuengde,
as *Cyrus* meanes for this *Libanio*.
                Exit omnes.

Enter Araspas, and a Magitian, to Panthea
a sleepe.

Ara. Giue me the charme, for now doth *Panthea* sleep
If it preuaile this iewell shall be thine,

Mag. Doubt not the operation of this charme,
For I haue tride it on *Dianas* nymph,
And made her wanton and lasciuious,
If *Panthea* be a Goddesse she must yeeld.

Ara. But tell me first, how must it be applied?
And in what time will it begin to worke?

Mag. Lay it vnder the pillow of her bed,
and in an houre it will make her wake and yeeld.

Ara. I will. Now fauour me infernall *Ioue.*

Mag. So, wake her not till she begins to smile,
Now loue begins to seaze him in her braine.

Pan. Away I will not, you are impudent.

Ara. Tell me Magitian, what importes this speech?

Mag. Why now she thinkes some solicites her.

Pan. You are deceiude, I am not beautifull.

Ara. O giue me leaue to court her in her sleepe,
It may be when she wakes she will not loue.

Mag. Softly Araspas, if you talke, she wakes.

Ara. O let her wake, I long to talke with her.

Mag. Now ginnes her eyes to open, and she stirres.

Ara. Stand thou aside vntill I call for thee.

Pan. What dreames and fond illusions haue I had?
How comes this word Loue, In *Pantheas* minde?
I loue, nay rather will I die then loue,
and yet against my will I thinke on loue,
O *Panthea* thinke vpon thy funerall,
For thou art withered with excessiue griefe,
Loue and deformitie cannot agree.

Ara. If *Panthea* be faire and beautifull,
Then loue and *Panthea* doe well agree.

D 3   Araspas

Pan. *Araspas*, *Panthea* and her felfe will iarre,
when fhe fhall yeeld to loue. Or what is loue
But gall and aloes to my martyred foule,
Now Abradates is not in my fight.

Araf. Here is Araspas louelie Panthea,
For thee Ile leaue the field, then leaue thou him,
For thee Ile leaue the world, then loue thou me.
Let Cyrus ioy in pompe and emperie,
Sufficeth me to conquer faire *Panthea*,
Let others glorie in their ground and golde,
Panthea to me is twentie thoufand worlds.
And without *Panthea* all the world is trafh,

Pan. For thee Araspas will I curfe my ftarres,
That fuffers thee fo to folicite me,
For thee I will count the world as hell,
Except thou leaue thus to folicite me.

Ara. How figuratiue is *Panthea* in her fpeach?
Refembling cunning Rethoritians,
who in the perfon of fome one deceafde,
Perfwades their auditors to what they pleafe,
I cannot thinke that thefe be *Pantheas* words,
She is fo faire to giue fo fharpe replie.
But if thefe be the wordes of *Panthea*,
Then muft fhe change her face, and feeme leffe faire,
For know that beautie is loues harbinger,
Then being beautious, *Panthea* needes muft loue.

Pan. Would I were changde into fome other fhape,
That I might fright thee with my hideous lookes,
I in the perfon of my felfe deceafde,
Proteft this heart fhall neuer harbour loue.
But if my lookes be this preparatiue,
Ile beate my face againft the haplesse earth,
Or deeply harrow it with thefe my trembling hands,
which I hold vp to heauen to chaunge thy minde,
Or haften death to rid me from this fute.

Nay

Araſ. Nay then if amorous courting will not ſerue,
Know whether thou wilt or no Ile make thee yeeld,
Pan. Though fortune make me captiue, yet know thou
That *Pantheas* will can neuer be conſtrainde.

Ara. But torments can enforce a womans will.

Pan. Then ſhould thy importunitie enforce,
The ſight of thee Araſpas ſhould conſtraine,
For I proteſt before the gods of heauen,
No torment can be greater in my thought.

Ara. I, ſay ſo till ye feele them *Panthea.*

Pan. I feele more torments then thou canſt inuent,
who adde the more ſhall eaſe that I ſuſtaine,
All torments be they neuer ſo exquiſite,
Are but aſcending ſteps vnto my ende.
And death tu *Panthea* is a beneſite,
what are thy threates but ſugred promiſes.

Ara. Then ſhalt thou liue and Ile importune thee.

Pan. I, now is *Panthea* menaced to the proofe.
Yet euery word thou ſpeakes ſhall wound my heart,
And in deſpite of thee Ile die at laſt,
The earneſter thou art the ſooner too,
But to preuent it thus I will flie from thee,
Cyrus ſhall know Araſpus villanie.

Exit Panthra.

Ara. Thus therefore ſhall I pine, abandou loue,
O t'is inherent to Araſpas ſoule,
And thereby claimes an immortalitie.
So it ſhall nere begin, nor neuer end,
A curſed Magitian, are theſe thy wicked ſpels?

Ma. O pardon me my honourable Lord,
For *Pantheas* vertues fruſtrated all my art.

Ara. Muſt Magicke yeeld to vertue? wherfore then
Didſt thou aſſure me ſhe ſhould be in loue?

Ma. So was ſhe being aſleepe, as did appeare.

Ara. And why not being wake, ſpeake villain ſpeake
Reaſon

Mag. Reason my Lord was the predominant,
Her intellectuall part striued against loue,
and Magicke cannot cominaund the soule,
while appetite and common sense remained,
You saw I made her smile, embrace the aire,
and shew the affects of amorous conceits,
Few women vse to skirmish with such thoughts,
and had this *Panthea* beene at libertie,
she would haue yeelded to your honours suite.
But in captiuitie is nought but greefe,
and loue with greefe will keepe no residence.

Ara. Smooth are thy wordes, but rough and harsh
    thy sense,
For they import *Panthea* cannot be forced:
Canst thou with inchauntations make her die?
That she being gone my loue may follow her.

Mag. Life is adiunct vnto our humane forme,
Exempt from Magicke and Magitians,
And that's the cause we sooner hurt brute beasts,
Then such as haue the semblance of our selues.

Ara. Deceitfull Artisan thy words are sleights,
Thy wordes deceitfull and full of guile,
Wit is a witch, sweete words must conquer her,
Out of my sight, yet conceale this attempt,
If thou bewray it, maugre all thy skill,
This sworde shall send thee to eternall hell.

                                        Exeunt.

        Enter Dinon and Libanis.
Dinon. Now are we at the bankes of Euphrates,
Farre from the campe where souldiers haunt,
and here may we vnder this poplar shade,
Discourse vpon the sweetnesse of our loue.

    Lib. You know my Lord I am too yong to loue,
    Dinon. Faire Alexandra, if thou loue not me.
  Thou art compact of adamant and yron,

                                              Thy

King of Persia.

Thy yeares are fit for loue, so are thy lookes,

Lib. How fit so ere my yeares be and my lookes,
I Alexandra am ynfit to loue.
Is not my father with the Persian king,
And I Alexendra as captiue in his stead,
And giue me leaue to waile my hard estate,
and make a riuer with my flowing teares,
That mingled with the streame of Euphrates,
May swiftly runne vnto my fathers seate,
And make him hast to great Antiochus.

Dinon. Nay rather sit vpon this sedgie bankes,
That I seeing thy shadowe in the streame,
May feede my fancie with thy pleasant view,
If not enioy the sweetnesse I desire,
and leape into the waues and drowne my selfe,
That thou maist pittie *Dinon* being dead.

Lib. O I could pittie *Dinon* being aliue,
But that I feare my father will not come,
and then shall Alexandra suffer death,
and being dead *Dinon* may pittie me.

Dinon. Loue, may I call thee loue, loe shee doth not
Her lookes giues warrant for that Epitite, (frowne,
For thee Ile kneele before Antiochus,
and rather then thou shalt be toucht by him,
Ile beare thee hence as farre as Tanais,
Or keepe thee close in these Assyrian woods.

Lib. No place is secrete to Antiochus,
Dost thou not know that kings hath reaching hands?

Dinon. I do yet know my sworde is sharpe and keene
which when I drawe and brandish in the aire,
all Babylon will fight in my auaile,
who honour me more than Antiochus,
I will not say how great thy dowre shall be,
Nor boast what cities I commaund,
Let this, though not a king in name,

In

In wealth and friends I am an Emperour.

Lib. If I should yeeld your honour might suppose,
That dignitie and wealth should conquer me,
Therefore I blush to say I loue my Lord.

Dinon. And when thou blushes *Dinons* heart is fired,
Therefore to quench it giue a gentle grant.

Lib. My honor being preserude, my grant is giuen.

Dinon. Thereof am I as chairie as thy selfe,
And of thy loue as of my proper life,
O *Alexandra* thy wordes rauisheth me,
Lull me a sleepe with sweetnesse of thy voice.

Lib. Then shall my song be of my *Dinons* praise,
Sleepe *Dinon*, then *Libanio* draw thy sword,
And manly thrust it in his slumbring heart.
There is no way to saue thy life but this.
And therefore feare not, shall I slaughter him
That intertained me with such amorous wordes,
Such bounteous gifts and golden promises?
When he shall know I am *Libanio*,
And go I cannot but I shall be taine,
Vnlesse I slay him in his haplesse sleepe,
For he will quickly wake and follow me,
Now *Dinon* dies, alas I cannot strike,
This habit makes me ouer pitifull.
Remember that thou art *Libanio*.   *She killes him.*
No woman but a bondman, strike and flie.

                                        Exit.

            Enter the Assyrian king and his Nobles.

An. Now that *Gobrias* fortresse is our owne,
His daughter prisoner, and his Countrie burnt,
Lets march from hence to welthie Babylon.
And muster those resolued Citizens,
To meete the Persian in the open field,
Twice hath he led his forces by our gates,
Yet neuer durst to mount his battring Ramme,

                                        Or

Or warlike engine against the rampred walles,
Therefore we lie no more in garrison,
But bustell out and fight for libertie,

Nob. My Lord behold where *Dinon* slaughtred lies

Ant. *Dinon*,thou art deceyde it is not he,

Nob. It is my Lord I know him by his scarres.

Ant. These scarres were giuen him in my fathers
dayes,
And now he is dead, ere I cou'd guerdon him.
The greatest honour I can doe thee nowe,
Is to lament and kisse thy huelesse cheekes,
And that will I performe for Dinons sake,
O that I could reuiue thee with this kisse,

Nob. Doubtlesse *Gobrias* daughter murdered him,
I sawe them in the morning walke abroad,
And since they ne're retuinde into the campe,

Ant. Then she hath done this execrable fact,
And so is fled vnto her traiterous sire,
O that a sillie Maide should slaughter him,
Which not a world of Persians could subdue,
Is there no ende of my calamitie?
My father done to death by *Cyrus* sword,
Wicked *Gobrias* and his daughter fled,
Falle *Cresiphon* resolude to murther me,
And now *Dinon* my chiefest captaine slaine,
Why runne we not vpon these Persians,
which are the authours of these miseries?
Come souldiers take him vp and march away,
Weele empire Babylon to meete our foes,
And be reuengde vnto the ninth degree,
Both of *Gobrias* and his familie. *Exeunt.*

Enter Cyrus, Pantea, Gobrias, Hystaspis,

Pan. O *Cyrus* if the fortune of thy hande,
Haue turnde my freedome to captiuitie,

And of a Queene made me a captiue dame,
Yet thinke that vertue is not thrall to chaunce,
Nor honour subiect to vnhappie time,
But like a gallant consecrated ship,
That in extreamest wrath and stormes of seas,
Vaunts all her sailes and fights the battaile out.

Cyr. Madame the reason of these vehement tearmes,
Cyrus doth neither know, nor can coniect,
If since the time of your captiuitie,
You haue not beene intreated as you ought,
The gods can tell t'is farre against my thought.

Pan. Then know my great Lord, the man that tooke
To gard my honor, and my person free, (the charge)
Long since doted on my person so,
That doting he hath sought my honors wreake,
A tedious siege (God knowes) I haue endurde,
More hedious vnto me then hastie armes,
While vilde *Araspas* with his lewde desires,
Ceaselesse solicited my vnlawfull bed,
Without repulses I haue quailed his hope,
Which he renued with charge of fresh assaults,
But my denials made his purpose vaine,
In fine, when no intreatie could preuaile,
To frame my fancie to his wicked will,
He falles to threatnings from perswasious tearmes,
And vowes to purchase his desires by force,
And therefore *Cyrus* (as thou art a king)
Protect a Ladies honour from the spoile,
And let thy bondmaid liue and die vnstaind,
And if there rest no other hope for me,
But hauocke wracke and ruine of my state,
O *Cyrus* on thy sworde let *Panthea* die,
And so preuent the daunger of my shame.

Cy. Ladie, how farre your vsage disagrees,
From *Cyrus* meaning, recorde be the gods,

A3

As for my ſelfe (not vainly be it ſaide)
I holde my eyes in bondage to my will,
And keepe my thoughts in yoke to reaſon loue,
My ſight on beautie neuer ſurfetted,
And where her beames were likely to infect,
My iudgement was a vaile before mine eyes
To beare ſuch pearcing fancies from my heart,
Such as I am, ſuch muſt my followers be,
Elſe let them packe they ſhall not follow me.
The man that offered to diſhonour you,
ſhall be ſo throughly chaſtiſed for his fault,
As you ſhall reſt ſufficiently reuenged,
and knowledge me a gracious conquerour,
Hiſtaſpis carie her to your pauilions

Pan. So ſtand the gods aſſiſtant to your armes,
as you ſtand pittifull to my miſhape.

        Exit Hiſtaſpis and Panthea.

Enter Gobrias, Libanio in womans attyre.
Lib. My Lord, the gods and fate reſerues your page,
To doe you further ſeruice ere he dies.
Cy. *Gobrias* giues your page in that attyre?
Go. My Lord, ſhe is no page of mine,
Some ſhameleſſe ſtrumpet and a laſcioious trull.
Lib. And hath my Lord forgot his ſeruant then?
Gob. Firſt muſt I know before I can forget,
Thee haue I neither ſeene nor knowne till now.
Lib. O ſay not ſo my Lord, for oft ere this
I haue beene ſeene and throughly knowne to you,
And you I knew to be my gracious Lord,
Gobrias that renowmde Aſſyrian.
Gob. Fond girle it ſeemes thy wits be not thine owne.
Lib. What hath my Lord forgot *Libanio?*
Gob. I know thee now thou art my ſweet *Libanio,*
Thy humorous habite made me to miſtake.

              E 2

I knowe thee nowe thou art my sweet Libanio,
A vertuous boy and of a noble spirit,
To whose deserts and courage I ascribe,
The rescue of my daughters libertie,
O Cyrus this is he that to preserue
My daughters freedome from the Assyrian king,
Chose to disguise himselfe in her aray,
In fearefull doubt and hazarde of his life,
To saue her honour from the tyrants wrath.

  Cyr. My boy, what ere thy birth and fortune be,
Great doth this mind and thoughts of honour taste,
Expressing markes of true Nobilitie,
And to excite thee to commended workes,
Which are the pathes that to aduauncement ledes,
Receiue this chaine of golde from Cyrus necke,
And weare it in the face of all the worlde,
Not as a fauor to thy person giuen,
But as in honour to thy vertuous minde.

  Lib. Great and surpassing is the kingly grace,
Yea farre beyond the compasse of my hope,
Gods grant me life and fortune to deserue,
This part of bountie at your royall hands.

              Enter Alexandra.

  Alex. Libanio then I haue not prayed in vaine,
Nor cal'de vpon the gods with fruitlesse vowes,
If thou once more be rendred to my sight,
The teares of whose supposed funerals,
Did houre by houre bedew my blubbered face.

  Lib. Madame, the blessing of my strange escape,
I attribute alone vnto the gods,
It past so farre the reach of humane sense.

  Alex. And for thy sake their aultars I will smoake,
With sweete perfume of thankefull sacrifice.

  Cy. But boy expres in breif what meanst thou minde

To scape so safely from th' Assyrian campe.

Lib. This meane I found and pleale my Lord & king,
vpon suppose of Alexandra selfe,
I was committed to a noble man,
Hight *Dimon*, to be guarded in his tent.
The glorie of my counterfeit attire,
And maners framed according therevnto,
Did so inflame *Dimon* that wish my loue,
That waking, sleeping, or what euer elfe,
He felt a restlesse combate in his thoughts,
In fine, more safely to commence his loue,
He led me quite beyonde th' Assyrian campe,
And brought me to the bankes of Euphrates,
Therefate we downe, and he with amorous plea,
Not onely fild, but cloyde my wearie eares,
lo farre that what with long continued talke,
And heate of sunne reflecting on the bankes,
Or happlies with the racking harmonie,
which Euphrates his gliding streames did keepe,
Which seeing I imagined that the gods
Had offred this occasion to my hands,
For sweete recouerie of my freedome,
Short tale to make, with dreadfull hand I drew,
The sworde that hangde loose dangling by his side,
And with the full of my extended force,
I sheathde it home amidst the owners ribbes,
He wounded fet an inwarde grone or two,
Then turning on his face breathes forth his life,
The deed dispatcht, I hied me thence amaine,
And scaping cleane, without impeach or stay,
Now stand before the Persian king this day.

Cyr. President of manly fortitude,
Exceeding farre the opinion of thy yeares,
Gobrias haue an honourable care,

Alex. Lehena now leaue Alexandras weedes,

That

That part is plaid, and be your selfe againe,
That part poore boy with danger thou hast plaid.
  Lib. Madame, no daunger can be so great,
That Ile refuse for Alexandras sake.
  Cy. Gobrias say, is Alexandra she,
For whom your page these hazards hath sustainde?
  Gob. It is my Lord. *Cy.* Then let vs to your wished for.
  Gob. That place O *Cyrus* I desire to see, (place.
  Cy. This is the place the men that follow me
  Gob. Then wample both my eyes that with this turfe,
I may be sure to hit a vertuous man.
  Cy. Shall she be his on whom this turfe shall light?
  Gob. So that the man be good and vertuous, and by
  Cy. Then throw at random when you please *Gobrias*,
You cannot misse a good and vertuous man.
  Gob. Then *Alexandra* at thy husbands head
  Cy. *Histaspis* you are hit. *Hist.* I am my Lord,
  Go. Then Alexandra if you please is yours,
  Hist. Happie were I if *Alexandra* please.
  Alex. My Lord the fortune of my fathers hand,
Becommeth not his daughter to withstand,
To please my Lord and father I am yours.
  Gob. Your fathers pleasde, *Histaspis* she is yours.
  Cy. Histaspis take your loue at *Cyrus* hand,
thus is our guise, and thus the Persians do,
they wooe and wed within a word or two: *Exeunt.*

Actus tertius.

Enter Antiochus, Hircanus, Aristobulus, and Ctesiphon.
  Ant. No *Ctesiphon* vnsheath thy bloodie sworde,
And shew it staind and cankred with the gore,
that issued from that vaunting Persians heart.
What draw man, and shew thy iust conceale,
thy pay is prest in readie numbred golde,
  Cte. My Lord and king I beare no bloodie sworde,
Nor staind with gore of Persians *Cyrus* heart.
  T

A

A prince he is farre from delite in blood,
Milde, lonely, vertuous, wise and bountifull,
Able to reconcile his greatest foes,
And make great princes of his meanest friends.

Ant. Thy going was to compasse *Cyrus* death,
How haps thy purpose ends without effect?

Cte. The Persian prince inclines to tearmes of truce,
and craues the friendship of Antiochus;
So please my Lord the king to firme a peace,
For briefe whereof his letters I present,
Signed and deliuered with his royall hand,
Sincerely tending to the same effect,
Whereto if once your highnesse condiscend,
He will withdraw his armies from Assyria,
And on the couenants seal de dissolue his campe.

Ant. In case the Persian prince be so inclinde,
thy answere shall lesse offend my mind.

Cyrus to Antiochus, health.
This bearer comming to my camp armd with resolution
to kill me, and is treated more honorably then either his
trecherie or thine could deserue. *Apprehend Ctesiphon.*

Cte. What reades my Lord aright, or doth he faine?

Hir. That you shall know before you start againe,
Vpon the instant purpose of his interprise, it pleased
God to confound him with such horror of conscience,
that vncostraind he cofest the treason; & intreated pardon, vowing himselfe so far forth friend to *Cyrus*, that
for his sake he would kill Antiochus. I was content to
sooth the man in his villanie, because I would haue thee
know the difference twixt an open fo, & a dissembling
friend, I giue thee this notice, not because I loue thee, or
regard thy life, but because a villain shall not triumph in
the murder of him whom I account an honorable conquest of my self. Reward him according to his merits; &
prepare to fight with me for thy own honor. *Farewell.*

This

The warres of Cyrus

Cre. Theis thanklesse Persian whom I spared from
Bequites me with the betraying of my life, (death.

Ant. What answere maketh traiterous *Ctesipho*?

Cre. O prince my guilt is plaine before my face,
And witnesse with a princes seale,
To stande vpon deniall were but vaine,
where open proofe conuicts me of offence,
I say no more, but prostrate at your feete,
Submit my selfe to mercie of my Lord,

Ant. Such mercie as to traitors doth belong,
Such, and no better *Ctesiph* shall finde,
Disarme him of his martiall abiliment.
Disgrade him of all titles of regarde,
And then referre his attachment to your prince,

Hir. This cote of armes, the badge of honor wun,
Through praise and vertue of thy auncestors,
We rent it from that traiterous backe of thine,
And as an honour stainde with villanie,
In deepe disdaine we stampe it vnder foote,

Arist. This sworde that once was girt vnto thy side,
To be employde in seruice of thy prince,
Now vowde to gore the bowels of his grace,
we breake it here vpon thy traiterous head,

Hir. These squares of knighthoode that present the
and honour due to chiualrie and armes, (pride.
whose prickes should force the proud couragious steed
with thundering race to breake the riders launce,
Thus doe we hew them from thy traiterous heeles,

Ant. Thou art no man of honour nor of armes,
Thou hast no title of Gentilitie,
Nor stile of honour left hereof to vaune,
But art become inferiour of regarde,
Then is the basest bondman of Assyria,
Or vilest slaue that haunties the Lydian dames,

Arist. Dishonoured traitor, now prepare thy selfe,

To

To yeeld thy head vnto the hangmans axe,
Cte. Not fate but my demerits makes me die,
O now I finde *Nullurum proditor*. *Exeunt*.

Enter Hiſtaſpes Araſpas.

Ara. I feare the furie of the Perſian prince,
Hiſtaſpis, Cyrus furie I doe feare,
Hiſt. And wrath of princes, what is it but death?
Araſpas on my honour make a proofe,
And neuer ſhunne the preſence of our Lord,
A prince he is moſt milde and mercifull,
Soone mollified with vowes and penitence,
And though with great impatience he endure,
Your threatned violence to the Suſan Queene,
Yet your ſubmiſſion and deſire of grace,
Will pearce him with compaſſion of your ſute,
And purchaſe pardon at his royall handes.
Aſa. O ſpitefull beautie that bewitcht my minde,
And led my fancie to ſuch foule extreames,
I will aſſay the mercie of my Lorde,
And yeeld my life to hazzard of his grace,
Hiſt. And doubt not but of Cyrus you ſhall finde,
A pitifull and paſing gracious prince.

Enter Cyrus.

Cy. Hiſtaſpis and the reſt, withdraw your ſelues,
Onely Araſpas ſtay behind with me.
Ara. My ſouereigne Lord in trembling feare I ſtay,
And proſtrate fall before your highneſſe feete,
The fraile affects and errours of my youth,
Enforſed through follies of a wanton will,
Hath caſt my life in perill of your wrath,
Blinded with charmes of beautie I haue falne,
And made my iudgement ſubiect to deſire,
And in purſute of loues vnbrideled rage,
I haue tranſgreſt the bounds of honours lawes,

F

O gracious Lord impute my error past,
Vnto the power of proud commanding loue,
That led my minde and thought so farre astray,
Forgiue those frailties of my youth, O king,
And take your seruant once againe to grace,
with feare of your displeasure almost slaine.

  Cy. Force to a Queene, and she a captiue too,
A Persian Lord so farre misled with lust,
Intend dishonour to a sillie dame,
Araspas they that would be conquerors,
Should chiefly learne to conquer their desire,
Least while they seeke dominion ouer others,
They proue but slaues and bondmen to themselues.
Now where are those your big and braue disputes,
Wherein you pleaded loue was voluntarie,
And fancieless and intertaind at will,
When you imbrace it in such raging heate,
That where intreaties faile of your desires,
You fall from vowes to violence with the dame,
Araspas for the excuse of this offence,
You find no president in Cyrus life.

  Ara. I know and grant my Lord, the prince abounds
with pearelesse gifts and graces of the minde,
wherewith the gods haue fild his kingly breast,
There nought but vertuous motions taketh roote,
Nothing but honour harbours in that seate,
And holy thoughts direct his royall deedes.
That so his grace might euerie way be found,
worthie the glorie of so hie a charge,
Yet since these frailties that disgrace your thrall,
are humane faults and incident to minde,
Where strong desires hold reason vnder yoke,
The wonted mercie of my Lord the prince,
So prone in fauour to the penetent,
May mittigate the shame of this my fault.

With ſweete compaſsion to his princes thrall.

Cyr. Araſpas I remit thee this amiſſe,
although blame worthie in the hieſt degree,
and for your tried deſerts in martiall praiſe,
I am content this follie to forget;
Yet would I haue it ſeeme vnto the world,
That my diſpleaſure made you flie from me,
And ſo reuolted to the Aſſyrian armes,
There this ſuppoſe ſhall make you intertainde,
and highly fauoured of that graceleſſe king,
By meanes whereoffull ſafely you may learne,
The garriſon and ſtrength of Babylon,
The vtmoſt force and puiſſance of our foes,
With euerie purpoſe of Antiochns,
The time and place where he intents to fight,
Then hauing learnde the full of euerie thing,
In ſecrete you may ſcape againe to me.
With iuſt relation of the Aſſyrian campe.
This ſeruice if you pleaſe to vndertake,
You ſhall effect a ſinguler good turne,
and reape mortall thanks at *Cyrus* hands.

Ara. No longer let Araſpas liue and breath,
Then with the vtmoſt venture of his life,
He will performe what *Cyrus* ſhall command.
And ſacred price for this extended grace,
Though in the compaſſe of this hard affaire,
I leaue th'Aſſyrian faction to maintaine,
yet vow to beare a truſtie Perſian heart.

Cy. Then go with fortune, and returne with health
and grant the gods this enterprice of thine,
May end and proſper with deſirde effect.

Ara. And grant the gods that *Cyrus* ſtill may liue,
happie in peace, and in armes victorious.

Cy. To pacifie the angrie *Panthea* moode,
I will perſwade her of Araſpas flight.

That

That he is reuolted to the Assyrian king.

Enter Panthea.

Pan. Readie the humble handmaid of my Lord.

Cyr. To talme the heate of your offended mind,
Thus haue I lost as braue a warriour,
As euer trode vpon the Persian fields

Pan. What warrior means my Lord and conqueror?

Cy. Araspas, who in feare of my displeasure,
Is fled from me vnto th'Assyrian campe,
And hath forsooke the Persians colours quite,
Thus madame for your sake hath *Cyrus* done,
Euen lost the worthiest souldier of his band.

Pan. Cyrus let not his losse perplex your minde,
If you will let me send a messenger,
Vnto my Lord and husband *Abradates*,
I know for these your princely fauours done,
To me his wife in this my captiues plight,
He will attend your fortune in the warres,
With more sincere affection, loue and zeale,
Then euer that vngracious person did,
Againe, my Lord my husband is a knight,
As forward treads, and fortunate in armes,
As euer spred his colours in the field.

Cyr. Is it likely Abradatus will forsake,
His natiue prince to follow forraine armes,

Pan. The father of this king by *Cyrus* slaine,
was highly loued and honourde of my Lord,
This now that reignes affected *Panthias* bed,
Sought to procure a most vniust diuorce,
Betwixt my best beloued Lord and me,
who therefore beares him an immortall hate,
The starres of which incurable dispight,
Remaine so deepe imprinted in his thought,
That ten times blessed would he thinke himselfe,
To finde a fit occasion for reuenge.

Beleeue

Cy. Beleeue me Madam, if your Lord be arm'd,
With ſuch fore grounded malice to the prince,
His helpe may greatly further my affaires,
And therefore if you can procure the man,
To ſtand aſsiſtant to the Perſian armes,
You ſhall deſerue great thankes at *Cyrus* hand.

Pan. *Cyrus,* I will preſume to make my Lord
A truſtie follower of the Perſian armes,
And him your highneſſe ſhall not faile to finde,
A noble friend and valiant gentleman.

Cy. And Madam, he ſhall want at *Cyrus* hands,
No praiſe, nor honour due to good deſerts. *Exeunt.*

Actus quartus.

Enter Antiochus, Araſpas, and Nobles.

Ant. *Araſpas* though thy birth and parentage,
Seeme deadly to the Aſſyrian eares,
Being diſcended of our chiefeſt foes,
who purchaſe gentrie by our ouerthrow,
And in their inſignes beare the Aſſyrian armes,
Yet ſeeing thou commeſt as confederate,
In token that I loue and honour thee,
Receiue this ſworde, and fight couragiouſly.

Ara. *Antiochus* Ile weare it for thy ſake,
And for the wrong that *Cyrus* offered me,
Vnleſſe my deſtnie preuent my drift,
Ile quicklie hanſell it with *Cyrus* blood.

Nob. Wherein hath *Cyrus* wrongd thee Perſian ſay.

Ara. In barring me of her whom I eſteeme,
Aboue the value of his Diademe.
Panthea my Lord.

Ant. What *Panthea,* Abradates wife?

Ara. I louely *Panthea* Abradates wife.

Ant. Speake not of *Panthea* if thou loueſt me,

For

For her remembrance wounds my heart afresh,

Nob. His grace is alwayes passionate and sad,
If she be mentioned, therefore name her not.

Ara. Not that alone, but manie iniuries,
Incenst me to attempt his ouerthrow,
For in the field wherein your father fell,
I got rich armour, golde, and sumptuous tents,
all which he tooke vnto his proper vse,
and gaue vnto his speciall fauourites,
Nor had I wherewithall at *Cyrus* hands,
To heale those wounds which I receiued in fight.

Ant. Then see thou make as deepe wounds in his
And so crie quittance with the couetous king, (flesh,
I giue thee to this sword, armour and horse,
a horse as fierce as proude *Bucephalus*,
armour of trustier proofe then *Thetis* found,
Therefore *Araspas* fight couragiouslie.

Ara. Albeit I haue not *Alexanders* skill,
To manage him, nor yet *Achilles* armes,
to charge as brauely, yet as good a heart,
as *Alexander* or *Achilles* euer had.
And when I shrinke for feare out of the field,
Let me be torne in peeces with that horse,
Or hewed to death with this bright cortelaux,

Ant. Thy wordes *Araspas* tise me to the field,
and makes me thinke I shall be conquerour,
Come let vs march from wealthie *Babylon*,
and then towards *Cyrus* with our royall campe. *Exeunt*

Enter Panthea, and Cyrus.

Pan. My husband mightie Lord, from *Bactria*,
Where he lay legar for th' *Assyrian* king,
Is come to serue vnder your highnesse flagges,
and in your aide hath brought two thousand horse,
Backt by his friends *Assyrian* Gentlemen.

al

all which will die at conquering *Cyrus* feete.

Cy. Is Abradates come from Bactria,
Then will I leaue to mone Araspas losse,
and thinke on conquest and sweete victorie?
Gobrias go with louely *Panthea*,
and bring him presently vnto our tent,
With those braue horsemen of Assyria,
You warlike and victorious men,
Marshall your seuerall bandys in equipage,
That Abradates king of Susia,
May wonder at the hugenesse of our campe,
and be the willinger to league with vs.

Enter Abradates with other.

Here he comes, and if by his aspect,
I may conjecture of his qualities,
He is valiant, wise, trustie and liberall,

Ab. I need not aske which is the Persian king,
The vertues shining in his glorious lookes,
Say this is Cyrus, and in signe of loue,
will Abradates thus salute his grace,

Cy. Sweete Abradates thou imbrasing me,
Hath stolne my heart, I loue and honour thee,

Ab. Faire Lord was neuer captiue gentler vsde,
Then *Panth:* of this gracious conquerour.
For Panthea, Cyrus I and this my traine,
Of which the meanest Soulder may take charge,
and be commander of a campe of men,
So able, wise and venterous they are,
Doth rest for euer at your highnesse becke,
Our horse which are grasing on the plaine,
In winter gallops, and in Isie seas,
and in the sommer swimmes the deepest streames,
Swifter are they in pace then lightfoot Hart,
Surer they are then Cammels dlodding on the waies,
Fiercer then Tygres, and as

Olephants

Olephants with Castles on their backes,
And if they were compast with arming pikes,
They knew which way to make their passage forth,
And when their sides is painted eke with blood,
they pull their reines, and lookes downe to the ground
As if they vaunted of their seruice done,
The rider being dismounted they stand still,
And kneele vpon the ground to take him vp,
But if he chaunce to die, they pine to death:
These are Cyrus and the riders too,
Souldiers as good as euer sunne behelde.

   Cyr. These horses thou speakest of makes me glorie
Then Lydian Cressus in his heapes of gold, (more,
And of them all doth Cyrus make account,
As of the strengthes and sinewes of the warre,
We haue intelligence the Assyrian king
Is come from Babylon to meete vs straight,
Therefore if Abradates fauour vs,
Mount and away for we'le assaile them first.

   Abra. For that comes Abradates, lets away.

   Pan. But Abradates I will arme thee first,
Seest thou these pouldrons they are golde,
These vanbraces and currets massie golde,
The gorget and thy helmet beaten golde,
The belt imbrodered golde, yet all to base,
For Abradate louelier then the golde,
May neuer speare be broken on this breast,
But that the point thereof may soone returne,
And strike him dead that durst to giue that charge,
This helmet shunne thee from the sling and darts,
This kisse make thee turne with victorie.
As for this garland made of loftie palme,
Panthea reserues it for her conquering Lord,
Vpon whose head will Panthea fasten it,
And hanging on his necke like Hectors wife,

                           Inquire

Inquire the maner of the battell past.

Abr. Faire be my fortune for my *Panthea*,

Hst. My Lord Araspas in th'Assyrian armies,
Doth craue successe vnto your Maiesties.

Cyr. Araspas, let him come, he is our friend.
And brings vs tidings from our enimies.

Enter Araspas.

Ara. Health vnto the person of my gracious lord.

Cyr. Welcome Araspas, bringe thou chearful newes
Is Antiochus resolued to fighte

Ara. This day he determines to encounter with your Host.

Cy. What is the number of his fighting men?

Ara. In all two hundred thousand at the least,
And thus in order lies his noble campe.
The forefront is entrabattou,
Of purpose to disranke the approching foe,
Next them are fiftie thousand horsemen placde,
To breake in where the chariots breake the way,
Next them fiue thousand slaues being lightily
laden with speares, helmes, naked swordes,
To go along to serue the horsmens vse.
Then twentie thousand Scythians ranagates,
with venomde darts, whose heddes are tipt with steele,
And last the battell of th'Assyrians,
Being hedgde with launces as a wood with Briers.
On whose heades the crossebowes and the slings,
will shoote and throw bullets of massie yron,
Whose verie fall would strike Antiochus downe,
In middest whereof Antiochus will march,
Before whom doe a thousand bondmen draw
A brazen wall built vpon turning wheles.
To gard him sure and his concubine,
All these vpon my honour I auer.

Cy. If euery souldier had a wall of brasse,
It could not daunt vs, we are resolute,

                    G   And

And vowed and sworne vnto our swordes;
which teacheth vs to scorne a brazen wall.

Abr. Renowmed *Cyrus*, honour me thus farre,
To haue the leading of your vauntgard forth.

Hist. Nay it belongs vnto a Persian.

Ara. If to a Persian, it belongs to me.

Hist. I serued Astiages your highnesse sire.
But if a stranger may deserue the place,
I hope my seruing merits it my lord.

Pan. My husband is a king, *Cyrus* I hope
will therefore grant it, if not for desert.

Cy. Had I foure to encounter with,
you all should lead the vauntgard of the field,
But onely one must haue the charge,
Though all deserue it, therefore draw you all.

All. Content.

Cy. Crysantas make the lots.

Hist. pardon me *Cyrus* though I do repine,
why should we draw lots for our proper right?

Cy. Ile haue it so, *Histaspis* be content.

Cry. The lots are readie.

Cy. *Histaspis* I command thee to begin,
Now *Abradates* and the rest.

Abr. Fortune hath fauoured me, the lot is mine.

Cy. Then thou shalt lead the forefront, let vs march.

Ara. The enemie is neare, make haste my Lord.

Cy. Here Abradates, Cyrus placeth thee,
Leade warily, and fight contagiouslie.

Abr. As mine owne life so tender I these men,
Now to the battell, *Panthea* Farewell. *Exeunt.*

Enter Panthea and Nicasia.

Pan. Farewell, and may good angell follow thee,
And euerie starre that raigned when I was borne,
Whose influence hath kept me yet from harme,

Vnfortunate

Vnfortunate be to make thee bleft.

Ni. And miferie ceafe on *Nicafia*,
So *Abradates* be kept from harme.

Pan. Ye Perfian Deities for *Cyrus* fake,
Affyrian Gods for *Abradates* fake,
Giue victorie vnto the Perfians,
That I may fee my husband weare this wreath.

Ni. Madam, Bellonas fhrine is heare at hand,
O let vs go to offer facrifice,
To make her more propitious to his grace,
For now he is amongft th'Affyrian troupes.

Pan. Ile offer all my iewels on the fhride,
And make fweet fumes of Ambergreece and Myrrhe,
Of Indian Caffia, Muske and Frankinfenfe,
That Abradates may be conquerour,
Firft at her aulter let vs ioyfully fing,
For Mufícke is a facrifice to her.

Affos quintus.

Enter Cyrus, Pambia, and the armie.

Pan. Great lords to whom the Affyrian fcepter yeelds
and Babylon through right of victorie,
Lies open to thofe conquering fwords of yours,
How fares my lord, my lord and louing feere,
My Abradates, liues he conquerour,
Or left by deftnie numbred with the dead.

Cy. Faire Ladie, vertuous, chaft and amiable,
I truft your lorde among the liuing dwels,
and like a champion and a knight at armes,
will fhew himfelfe or mine houres expire,
His temples adornde with victorious palme.

Pan. When to the fight my lord adreft his bands,
Deuoutly attired I Belonas farine,
And there before the aultar of the Saine,
Perfumde the ayre with fmoke of holie fire,

G 2   And

And breathed forth my plaints and eke my moanes,
Thrice I me seemed the Goddesse turnde her face,
Offending-like frowning with angrie browes,
Againſt my prayers and my holie vowes,
O Cyrus, if my iealous thoughts diuine,
Some diſmall ſequell to this fantaſie,
Yet pardon me ſeeing womens wittes are weake,
And loues aboundes with ſuperſtitious feare.
  Cy. Madam, I truſt the preſence of your Lord,
Returning backe in triumphant renowme,
Shall ſoone remoue thoſe thoughts out of your mind,
So graunt the Gods my countries preſidences,

Abradates borne in dead.

  Cy. What ſlaughtered bodie do you Perſians bring?
  Captain. Cyrus the bodie of the Suſian king,
Scout Abradates by the Egyptians ſlaine.
  Pan. Now let my Lord the prince of Perſia iudge,
whether vnhappie Panthea ſeared me vaine,
O noble loue whoſe manly heart deſerude,
To ioy the benefite of longer life,
And richer Trophes to enlarge the ſame:
But tell vs now after what ſort he died?
  Cap. Mounted aloſe his chariot armed with ſithes,
Beating the ſtrong Egyptians downe,
A few of his faithful truſtie friends,
With dreadfull race inſiſt his chariot Wheeles,
While the other in the battaile turning backe,
Abandoned him among the Egyptian pikes,
Yet Abradates with the few remained,
By force and vertue of his puiſſant hand,
Sendes thouſand of the heathniſh foes to hell,
Till at the laſt diſmounted from his ſeate,
And round enuironed with his enemies,

After so many mortall wounds receyued,
He fell and yeelded vp his kingly ghoſt.
The Egyptians as their barbarous cuſtome is,
when he was dead cut off his ſtout right hand,
And left it lying by the breathleſſe corps:
But with a band of Perſian men at armes,
we reſcued him and brought him to your grace.
Here to receiue ſuch worthie funerals,
As fits the honour of ſo great a Lord.

Pan. Now Euphrates whoſe ſad and hollow bankes,
Haue ſuckt the ſumme of *Abradates* blood:
which from his wounds did iſſue with his life,
Now ceaſe thy courſe of thy diſdained teares,
And let thy courage turne againſt the tide,
Of mere remorſe of wretched *Panthea* plaints,
Is this the hand that plighted faith to me,
The hand, that aye hath managde kingly armes,
And brought whole troops of mightie warriors down,
Now ſeuded from the bodie of my Lord,
Cleane voide of feeling, ſenſe and vitall breath,
So Gods and cruell deſtnies commaund,
Malignant of poore *Panthea* happineſſe.
Liue *Cyrus.* You Lords of Perſia,
Command my honour to poſteritie,
That ages hence the world report may make,
That *Panthea* died for *Abradates* ſake.

She ſtabs her ſelfe

Nic. Gone is my Ladie peerleſſe *Panthea,*
Slaine with ſelfe griefe for *Abradates* ſake,
Nicaſia loathes to liue when ſhe is gone,
The pride and Phenix of Aſſyria,
Ile not preſume to touch the fatall ſteele,
Wherein my Ladies ſacred blood do ſmoake,
Receiue me in thy bowels Euphrates,
And let thy bottome be *Nicaſia* graue.

Enter

The warres of Cyrus

Enter Cyrus, Araspas, and Gobrias, to Abradates dead.

Cy. O Persians see if any breath remaineth.

Ara. Cyrus, alas all sense of feeling is gone,
His senselesse lims with stiffenesse ouergrowne,
No rubbing warming, ought auaileth vs,
But pale death sits as conquerour ouer him.

Let Araspas kneele downe by Abradates.

Cy. Mirrour of honor and true Nobilitie,
No age, no time shall euer race thy fame,
Whilest Euphrates doth keepe his running streame.
What Abradates, and chast Panthea too,
O Abradates worthie man at armes,
O Panthea chast vertuous and amiable,
This office Cyrus to your wandring ghost,
Reserues in store to grace your funerals,
with monuments of fatall Elonie,
Of Cedar, Marble, Iet, and during brasse,
That future worlds and infants yet vnborne,
May kisse your tombes wherein your bodies lie,
And wonder at the vertues of your minde,
Assyrian Lord, such honour thou shalt haue,
As neuer had Assyrian at his graue.
Six hundred head of cattell shall be slaine,
And sacrificed vpon the funerals day.
Twelue thousand horses being manned each one,
Trapt all in blacke shall goe before thy hearse,
The towred battlements of Babylon,
Bend in contempt of heauen and earth, and men,
Those markes of pride shall be abated downe,
To make a shew of mourning for thy death.
Such honour as you both receyude in life,
Such honour shall you both receiue in death.

FINIS.

PR
2411
W2
1594a

The wars of Cyrus

PLEASE DO NOT REMOVE
CARDS OR SLIPS FROM THIS POCKET

UNIVERSITY OF TORONTO LIBRARY

ImTheStory.com

Personalized Classic Books in many genre's

Unique gift for kids, partners, friends, colleagues

Customize:

- Character Names
- Upload your own front/back cover images (optional)
- Inscribe a personal message/dedication on the
  inside page (optional)

Customize many titles Including
- Alice in Wonderland
- Romeo and Juliet
- The Wizard of Oz
- A Christmas Carol
- Dracula
- Dr. Jekyll & Mr. Hyde
- And more...

Lightning Source UK Ltd.
Milton Keynes UK
UKHW022016110220
358552UK00015B/277